Praise for *Being the Strong Ma*

A must read for men who feel they have compromised themselves and aren't getting the response they expected, and for women who wish they were in a relationship with a real man. This book illuminates an essential foundation upon which a healthy relationship can be built.

– Aryeh Pamensky, Director of the Pamensky Relationship Institute, Author of *How to Make a Good Marriage Great!*

A brave and creative attempt to pass on the wisdom of strength without harm, wisdom that was once part of the training of gentle, strong and loving manhood in a thousand cultures more subtle and skillful than our own. To be strong does not mean dominating. Only when a man and a woman are both strong, can they be truly close.

– Steve Biddulph, Author of *The Secret Life of Men, Raising Boys, The Secret of Happy Children* and *The Secret of a Happy Family*

An insightful book about one of life's most important goals: How a man can be a hero to his wife.

– Shmuley Boteach, Author of *Kosher Sex, The Private Adam* and *Kosher Adultery*

A cautionary tale, it cautions us to not throw out the baby with the bath water – to not toss out the man with the insensitivity.

Offers hope to men and women alike – A must read for every man who is ready to reclaim his masculine self and start becoming the kind of man that a woman really wants.

What type of man are strong women longing for? A strong man. In a very sensitive way, Elliott Katz teaches us a lot about this difficult matter. It is a lot of fun reading this book.

Practical, wise and common sense guidance on what it takes to succeed in our most important relationship. What a simple and obvious truth; it takes effort and taking responsibility – the traits of a "strong man."

Finally – a book for men in their unique role in marriage! This book breaks new ground as it offers a fresh philosophy and the practical techniques for implementing it. It will help those men who have found themselves stuck in outmoded conceptions of masculinity — including both the old fashioned "man's man" and the feminized male of recent decades.

– Sarah C. Radcliffe, M. Ed. Psychological Associate,
Member of College of Psychologists of Ontario, Author of
Aizer K'negdo – the Woman's Guide to Marriage and
The Delicate Balance — Love and Authority in Parenting

Elliott Katz does an excellent job of presenting many of the essential challenges couples face, and in particular, what is the correct way for the man to respond. He presents his "teachings" with a charming simplicity that is sure to warm the hearts of many readers. His notion that the man needs to be an emotionally strong and mature partner is certainly in order and proven in my clinical practice as a seasoned marriage and family therapist to be true over and over again. Katz's book is eminently practical and down to earth. It is sure to be received enthusiastically by many who need to learn the basics of how to make a marriage work.

– Abraham Kass, M.A., R.S.W., R.M.T., Clinical Social Worker,
Member of the Ontario College of Social Workers, and the Ontario
and American Association for Marriage and Family Therapy

This book shows how men (and women) can not only survive in a foreign, enemy, alien territory called marriage, but actually thrive in it! The best part of the book is that I couldn't put it down....a fast and fun read...my wife just nodded her head and smiled wryly when we discussed the issues together. I recommend this book to anyone who is married or wanting to marry – to avoid the heartbreaking consequences of becoming a divorce statistic. Get this book into the hands of every man!

– Mark J. Halpern, CFP, FMA, Marriage Coach, Adult Education Teacher

Mandatory reading for current or future husbands!

– Dr. Mark Schwartz, MBA, LLB, PhD, Lecturer, Business Ethics, Schulich School of Business York University

Time-proven wisdom from the sages that challenges many of the behavioral norms that have emerged over the past thirty years.

– Robert Gordon, Economist

This book will awaken the brilliance of all men who want a successful and happy relationship.

– Pamela Sims, M. Ed., Author of *Awakening Brilliance: How to Inspire Children to Become Successful Learners*

Rightly points out that growth and maturity ensues from taking responsibility – the ideas revealed in this story will help bring peace between men and women.

– Dr. Jonathan Evan Siegel, Psychologist

I was surprised to learn the word "husbandship" is defined in the dictionary. It's a powerful message.

– Hesky Green, Software Engineer

Being the
STRONG MAN
A Woman Wants

Being the
STRONG MAN
A Woman Wants

Timeless wisdom on being a man

Elliott Katz

Award Press

Award Press
www.awardpress.com
Email: bethestrongman@aol.com

Printed in Canada
10 9 8 7 6 5 4 3

Katz, Elliott
    Being the strong man a woman wants : timeless wisdom on being a man / Elliott Katz.
Includes bibliographical references.
ISBN-13 978-0-9736951-0-6

    1. Men—Life skills guides. 2. Men—Psychology. 3. Masculinity.
I. Title.

HQ1090.K375 2005   646.7'0081   C2004-906687-0

Cover and interior design by Tinge Design Studio

Cover photo from Firstlight.ca

This book is available at special quantity discounts for bulk purchases for educational purposes, premiums, sales promotions, fund-raising, special books or gift-giving.

Disclaimer — Please Read This!

The author has done his very best to give you useful and accurate information in this book. He cannot guarantee that the information will be appropriate to your particular situation. If you are having problems, consult the appropriate professional. The author and publisher shall have neither liability nor responsibility to any person with respect to any loss or damage caused, or alleged to be caused, directly or indirectly by the information contained in this book. We assume no responsibility for errors, inaccuracies, omissions or any other inconsistencies herein. Any slights against people or organizations are unintentional. If you do not wish to be bound by the above, you may return this book to the publisher for a full refund.

Contents

A woman wants a strong man

By Robert A. Glover Ph.D.

What do women want? An age-old question, but one of significant relevance to every 21st century male. The last 50 years have brought a shift in gender roles and relationship expectations. Men have been told they must learn how to please women and evolve beyond the patriarchal stereotypes of their forefathers. But no matter how hard he works at trying to please women, the path of the sensitive new age guy is strewn with frustration, bewilderment and resentment.

What do women want? A healthy woman wants a strong man, a man who can make a decision, a man who can be depended on, a man who can look out for the best interests of his loved ones, a man who does the right thing – not the easy, popular or expedient thing.

What do women want? Elliott Katz has hit the nail on the head in his provocative and ground-breaking book, *Being the Strong Man a Woman Wants*. Drawing from the wisdom of the ages, Katz guides the reader through the labyrinth of confusion created by today's "enlightened" thinking on gender roles. Drawing upon age-old principles that work, Katz shows the modern male how to be the kind of man that women want without regressing into authoritarian, abusive, or controlling stereotypes of masculinity.

Being the Strong Man a Woman Wants is a book that offers hope to men and women alike. It is a must read for every man who is ready to reclaim his masculine self and start becoming the kind of man that a woman really wants.

– Robert A. Glover Ph.D., Author of *No More Mr. Nice Guy: A Proven Plan for Getting What You Want in Love, Sex and Life*

The story behind the journey

When there's a problem in our relationships, it's often easier to blame than to take responsibility. However at some point, we have to realize the relationship is a mirror and these challenges are opportunities for our own personal growth. But how do we learn what we need to know in order to grow? Television and movies offer confusing ideas and stereotypes.

When I began my journey, I wondered if I was the only one to have faced some of these challenges. Since men and women have been involved with each other for thousands of years, I wondered: Isn't there some wisdom that I can learn from? I started searching and found refreshing insights that spoke directly to me.

I learned that for thousands of years men have learned wisdom from other men on dealing with these challenges. Contrary to many of today's clichés about men, this wisdom tells men to be strong and what it means to be strong – the opposite of controlling. It tells men about the noble qualities, admirable traits and virtues of being manly. I discovered that for many years men have dealt with and grown from similar challenges that men face today.

In this story, a grandfather connects his grandson to this timeless wisdom. This book isn't meant for everyone, yet I'm always amazed to find the number of people that it speaks to and helps to put on a path to being stronger and happier. I hope you enjoy the journey and that it leads you to greater happiness.

Elliott Katz

CHAPTER ONE

If you don't lead, I can't dance

Michael raised his glass to his grandfather, "Grandpa Joseph, to you and Grandma Sarah on your fiftieth anniversary. Tell me, how did you do it? Lisa and I have been together for seven years and I don't think we're going to make it to eight."

Grandpa put his hand on Michael's shoulder. "It wasn't easy. We both had a lot to learn."

"I've tried hard to be nice and make her happy. But no matter what I do, it's never good enough."

His grandfather nodded. "Michael, it's been a long time

since I've seen you. I'm glad you came. Today, let's enjoy the party. Tomorrow, just the two of us, we'll talk. How about a hike, like in the old days?"

Michael sighed. "I'll ask Lisa."

He thought about why he'd been late for the party. He had wanted Lisa and the kids to come, but she'd said no and didn't want him to go either. He couldn't understand why.

He had missed seeing Grandpa Joseph and Grandma Sarah's surprise when they arrived. He knew they had been expecting a quiet backyard picnic with Michael's parents, Norm and Helen. Instead, a long white banner with 50 AMAZING YEARS! in big red letters and the cheers of their children, grandchildren and great-grandchildren had welcomed them.

Michael watched his grandfather give candy to the younger children. With Sarah at his side, Grandpa then stepped forward to speak. He blinked back tears as he looked around at his family.

"It's hard to believe it's been fifty years," he said as he looked at Sarah. "When we met, I knew Sarah was the one for me. Her goodness and kindness matched her beauty. When we were first married, we struggled. We didn't have anybody to ask for help. But we kept going. When times were hard, Sarah always helped me to see the good."

Grandpa kissed Sarah on the cheek. She had changed little over the years. Her figure had matured and was now more rounded, but her face wore the same warm, welcoming smile she shared with everyone. Her dark hair was shorter and starting to gray. She dressed simply, as always, in a white blouse and a long blue skirt.

Everybody cheered and raised their glasses high. Michael took a sip of his wine, then looked over at his grandfather. He admired the way Grandpa had kept fit, his back and shoulders still straight. His deep blue eyes still held their glint. Michael hadn't realized before how much he looked like his grandfather. Both were six feet tall, with strong builds and wavy dark hair, but Grandpa's hair had streaks of gray.

Michael looked around at his family. It had been a while since he'd seen them, and it felt good to be back. He saw his dad Norm, Grandpa and Grandma's oldest son. His dad, also tall and broadly built, came over to greet him. "So how's the new job? How do you like being the publisher?" Michael smiled to himself. He knew his dad was proud of his success at work.

"They like my ideas. I'm really excited about it."

His mother Helen joined them. Petite and always glamorous, she was reveling in being hostess to so many people. "How are things with Lisa and the kids?" she asked.

"The same." Michael quickly changed the subject. "This

is a great party Mom. You've made Grandma and Grandpa very happy."

The music began to play a Viennese waltz, one popular when Joseph and Sarah were first married. As Michael walked across the backyard, he saw a dove land on the wooden fence and listened to its *chroo chroo*. He looked at the dove, then over at his grandma and went over to her. She'd always been one of his favorite people and she was the best cook in the world. Her door was always open.

"Michael, it's good to see you," Sarah smiled. She reached up and gave him a big hug.

Michael took her by the arm. "May I have this dance?"

She smiled and they walked onto the lawn where Michael led her in the sweeping turns of the waltz.

As they danced, Michael said, "Grandma, I heard a theory. They say being a couple is like dancing. When one person steps forward, the other steps back. Do you think it's true?"

Sarah thought for a moment. "I think it's like dancing in another way. If you don't lead, I can't dance."

CHAPTER TWO

Being strong

The next morning was bright and clear. Michael, dressed in hiking shorts and a T-shirt, drove to his grandparents' home. It was a small older house on a street lined with big leafy trees. He looked up at the thick branches and remembered how he used to climb them. Those were the good old days, he thought. He went into the kitchen through the back door.

Grandma Sarah was making breakfast and talking with her neighbor Leanna, a tall blonde who had recently separated from her husband David. She and Sarah were good friends and always had a lot to talk about.

"Come, sit down. Eat," Sarah said as she brought plates of eggs, toast and fruit to the table.

As always, she served Grandpa first. She's so old-fashioned, Michael thought.

Grandpa took a bite. "Sarah, it's delicious. You've outdone yourself again. Thank you."

Sarah beamed.

Michael smiled. Grandma was so appreciative of Grandpa's compliments. Grandpa ate quickly and excused himself. He said he had to find something.

As soon as Grandpa was out of the room, Michael asked, "Grandma, what's kept you and Grandpa together all these years?"

"He's a good man, a tower of strength."

Michael was surprised. "Does he talk about his feelings?"

"Feelings? Sometimes he does. But when I hear a man always talking about his problems, I shake my head. I want a man who is strong and sure of himself. It makes me feel safe and loved. It's hard to admire a man who always talks about his problems." Smiling to herself, she said, "It reminds me of something my mother said: 'A woman wants to admire and look up to her man, but she doesn't want him to look down on her.'"[1]

"Your mother was right," Leanna broke in. "I wish my

ex-husband had figured that out. He never understood that I may be a boss at work, but when I'm with a man I want to feel like a woman. I want him to be strong, to protect me. David is a good guy. He did things around the house, washed the dishes, changed diapers. But I felt like a single parent. When there was a decision to be made, he'd say, 'You decide.' I want a man who knows what he wants. I couldn't respect him. He didn't fulfill my emotional needs."

Michael looked uncomfortable. "Sounds like he's a nice guy. Maybe you didn't appreciate him."

"He is a nice guy, but I needed him to take charge. He wouldn't. Or couldn't. I had to be in charge and I resented it."

"You sound like my wife," Michael mumbled under his breath.

"Michael!" Leanna raised her voice in frustration. "You just don't get it. David didn't get it either. Nobody's going to ask you. You have to step up to the job."

"It should be a partnership," Michael defended himself. "Besides, what's wrong with being a nice guy?"

"Nothing, but I want a man who has backbone," Leanna said.

"You wanted him to control you?"

"There's a big difference between having backbone and being controlling."

"Leanna, it sounds like you want a knight in shining armor."

"A knight in shining armor wouldn't say 'You decide.'"

Sarah tried to calm things down. "Michael, do you know what they used to call men who let their wives run everything?"

"What?"

"Henpecked."

"Like the hen that laid these eggs?" Michael tried to make a joke.

Sarah and Leanna looked at each other. Leanna threw up her hands.

Grandpa was standing at the kitchen door listening. He was carrying a worn notebook.

"I found what I was looking for. Michael, hurry up and finish eating. Let's go."

She wants to admire and look up to you.
She wants you to be strong.

CHAPTER THREE

Knowing what you want

Michael and Grandpa walked out of the house and over to Michael's station wagon. They threw their knapsacks into the back, and with Michael at the wheel, headed north on the highway. After driving for an hour, they turned off onto Lookout Mountain Road. Michael had driven this route many times. He slowed down as the road followed the swift-flowing river through a narrow valley and gradually climbed to the entrance of Lookout Mountain Park.

Michael parked near the visitor center. He stepped out of

the car and breathed in deeply. The fresh air felt wonderful. He looked up at the rocky ridges, then closed his eyes and listened to the rapids in the river nearby. When Michael was younger, Grandpa had taken him on hikes here and taught him how to build a campfire.

They walked into the visitor center and over to a large wall-map showing the trails that began nearby.

"Let's do the Summit Trail to the top of Lookout Mountain. What do you think, Grandpa?" Michael asked. "It's got a great view."

"You're the guide." Grandpa said. "You decide."

"Okay, let's do it."

They went back to the car, got their knapsacks and started up the Summit Trail. Soon they were in a forest of tall white poplars that blocked the sunlight. The soft earth they walked on was such a change from the concrete of the city.

Michael paused, savoring the quiet. "Grandpa, I needed this walk."

"Sounds like you've got a lot on your mind. What's going on?"

"What am I going to do about Lisa?"

"What's the matter?"

Michael hesitated before answering. "She's always criticizing me. She says I don't do enough, but I do everything I can. She's turning the kids against me. I don't want to go home any more. I never know what's waiting for me. Even today I feel sick in my stomach thinking about it. I've been getting chest pains."

"This sounds so familiar, Michael. Let me tell you about my experience. Your grandma is a wonderful person. I'm lucky I married her and I've learned a lot being with her. Years ago I wasn't sure how to handle things at home and I let her run the show. She also said I wasn't doing enough. I realized when she said that, she meant I wasn't showing enough leadership. Some men are controlling and want to control all the decisions. I was the opposite. I was hardly making any decisions at all. I was leaving it to her and she wasn't happy. She didn't want someone controlling but she also didn't want someone who left her to run the show. Let me tell you what I learned. It's not the same for everybody. This worked for me and it may work for you."

"Go ahead."

"The first lesson I learned about making Grandma happy was I had to know what I wanted. I had to know how I wanted to handle things."

"What do you mean? I know what I want, but she's always disagreeing with me. Shouldn't it be a partnership?"

"I learned Grandma wanted to look up to me. She wanted me to be strong – not somebody who just wanted to please her. If I wasn't strong, if I didn't make decisions, she lost respect for me. Don't you lose respect for somebody who has no backbone?"

Michael didn't know what to think. He had shrugged off Grandma and Leanna for saying the same thing. If that was what Lisa wanted, why was she so against him?

They walked through the forest till they reached Crystal Lake. The glare of the sun reflected on the water, making Michael squint.

"Look, a loon!" Michael said, as they watched it dive into the water for fish.

"That loon knows what he wants," Grandpa said.

Across the lake, the cliffs of Lookout Mountain rose steeply from the water. Michael was eager to reach the summit.

"Let's keep going, it's great at the top." Michael led Grandpa along the trail on the lake's rocky shore.

Grandpa continued, "I learned what really mattered was guiding my family to the goals that Grandma and I set – even when I was tired after working all day."

"I try, but Lisa is so critical. If I make a mistake, she doesn't let me forget it. I keep giving in and I'm ready to give up. It's easier to just go along."

Grandpa nodded, "Michael, what you're saying isn't new. I used to think it would be easier to just go along with Grandma, that it would bring peace. But I was wrong. She didn't respect me."

"I thought going along with Lisa would make her happy and she'd appreciate me, but she doesn't."

"The irony is that if you're just always trying to please the other person, you don't really please her at all," Grandpa answered. "If you show her you know what you want, she'll respect you more."

"But I want peace."

"Is there peace now? Peace doesn't come from always giving in. Kids need to see their parents respect and support each other."

The trail reached a meadow where wild flowers were in bloom. Grandpa and Michael stopped to take in the glorious colors.

Grandpa chuckled and then began a story. "A car dealer told me that when a man and woman come in together, it's usually the woman who chooses the car they buy. One day he kept score. The first couple came in, the woman chose a car and the man went along. Next couple, same thing. And on and on it went till the sixth couple. The man told the dealer which car he wanted and the wife agreed."

"The dealer said to himself, at least one man took charge today. So he said to him, 'You made a good decision.'"

"The man looked puzzled and said, 'My wife told me what she wanted.'"

Michael laughed as Grandpa went on. "This has been going on for thousands of years. Do you know who Themistocles was? During the fifth century BC, he ruled Athens and laid the foundations of the Athenian empire.[2] He said, 'I govern the Athenians, my wife governs me.'"[3]

Michael nodded. "Mussolini, the dictator who ruled Italy during the Second World War – I read that his daughter said it was her mother who was the real dictator of the family."[4]

Grandpa smiled, "Sir Winston Churchill was the Prime Minister who led Great Britain to victory during the Second World War. He was a strong leader. In 1960, a newspaper reporter asked him about the prediction that in the year 2000, women will rule the world. Churchill said, 'They still will, will they?'"[5]

Michael chuckled. "Grandpa, is there any hope for us?"

"Churchill also said his most brilliant achievement was persuading his wife to marry him."[6]

She wants a man who knows
what he wants.
The irony is, if you're just
always trying to
please her, you don't really
please her at all.

CHAPTER FOUR

Leadership

Grandpa and Michael walked through the meadow. Michael breathed in the scent of the wild flowers. "We came at the best time of the year," Michael said as he savored the blues, reds and yellows of the wild flowers in bloom.

"When Grandma and I were starting out, we argued all the time. It seemed that everything I wanted, she wanted the opposite. I thought things would get better, but as time went on, they got worse." Grandpa sat down on a boulder and pulled out the old notebook he had packed that morning.

Michael's eyes opened wide in surprise, "Really? I always thought you and Grandma had one of those old-fashioned marriages that just worked."

"Grandma has a lot of good qualities, but I don't know any marriages that just work. I started looking for wisdom on what I could do to improve things, and whenever I learned something that made me say, 'I wish I'd known this,' I wrote it down in this notebook. The first thing I learned was that I wasn't the only one with these challenges. They've been going on for thousands of years."

Michael was beginning to feel a special connection with Grandpa that he hadn't ever felt before. "What's in the notebook?"

Grandpa opened it to the first page and took out a photo of his father. "I keep my father's picture here to inspire me. He taught me a lot – as much as my mother."

"Lisa does most of raising Danny and Jessica. I figure she knows more about it than I do. I bring in the money."

"You're not the first to think that." Grandpa turned to a page in his notebook and said, "You will have grief and misery if you think that money and property are enough to make you a true father of a family.[7] That's from Samson Raphael Hirsch in the nineteenth century."

Grandpa turned the page and went on. "There's an ancient Jewish custom of having a memorial service for relatives who have passed away. The part for remembering a father says, 'My father, my teacher.'[8] It doesn't say, 'My father, who paid for the stuff I wanted.'"

"Things are different today," Michael protested.

"Are they? How many people do you know who blame their problems on fathers who were hardly around?"

Michael didn't say anything.

"Do you remember Dr. Benjamin Spock?" Grandpa asked as he turned the page.

"Of course, my mom used his book Baby and Child Care to raise me. Back then, all mothers read Dr. Spock. It was one of the best-selling books of the twentieth century. I'd like to publish a book that sells like that."

"He also wrote a book called Dr. Spock on Parenting. In it, he said women complained to him that their husbands were reluctant to discipline their children. Dr. Spock said disciplining is not only teaching, it's 'leading, managing, training, correcting and in some cases punishment.' He thought some mothers were unfair because they wanted their husbands to be more stern than necessary, but he believed more were right – that their husbands were avoiding their share of leadership."[9]

"Leadership? He sounds like Leanna."

"Dr. Spock said that if a father 'is to have an ideal

influence on his children as well as a good relationship with his wife, he must be first of all a father, which means being a leader of and a model for his children.'"[10]

Grandpa kept reading. "'If a father shows himself to be only a good-natured, overgrown child, he deprives his son of a strong model to pattern himself after. He also deprives his daughter of a good male pattern on which to build her future relations with the whole male sex and particularly with her future husband.'"[11]

"Believe me, I've tried, but Lisa undermines me. I'm ready to give up."

"Listen, you're not the only one. Dr. Spock wrote about that too. He said, 'I've known cases in which a mother complained bitterly of her husband's failure to discipline, but when he tried to make some decisions for the children and to correct them, she tended to contradict him or to countermand his directions.'"[12]

"So what can I do?"

"Michael, you need to guide your children – to teach them right and wrong and how to deal with the challenges of life. You need to help them grow up. That's what fathers did for thousands of years. Things changed when men started leaving home to go to work."

"You mean when women left home to go to work, don't you?"

"No, I mean men. Fathers didn't always work away from home all day. That's not how it used to be. Not that long ago, people worked at home on a farm or in their own business. Fathers were able to be more involved as teachers and leaders of their families."

Grandpa continued, "As society became more industrial, big companies were set up. Fathers left for work early in the morning and came back exhausted at the end of the day. It was one of the most important changes in the history of the family.[13] Since then, children spend most of the day with their mother or with another woman who looks after them. Then they go to school where most of the teachers are women. And a lot of fathers relegated themselves to making money."

Thinking that a man's main job is to provide isn't new. In the nineteenth century, Samson Raphael Hirsch taught that a man will have grief and misery if he thinks money and property are enough to make him a true father of a family .

Dr. Benjamin Spock said that if a father "is to have an ideal influence on his children as well as a good relationship with his wife, he must be first of all a father, which means being a leader of and a model for his children."

CHAPTER FIVE

It's not being controlling

Grandpa and Michael continued walking through the meadow, each lost in his own thoughts. They entered a wooded area where the sunlight made the forest floor a lush green. Michael picked up the pace as they started climbing a long ridge on the side of Lookout Mountain. They reached a rock outcropping and hiked out on it to take in the view.

Michael pointed. "Look over there – that's the visitor center where we began. We've made good progress."

Then he turned to Grandpa and said, "What you're

saying is so different from what I've always heard. Isn't it being controlling?"

"Sounds like you believe all the terrible things you've heard about men – even the jokes that make fools of men."

Michael smiled. "Like, what's the difference between men and fine wine?"

"What?"

"Wine matures with age."

Grandpa sighed with a sour look on his face. He shook his head. "Most men I know are decent, mature people."

"I know. But aren't some men controlling?"

"Some. But don't confuse being strong with being controlling. Being strong is hard work. It's a burden. It's taking responsibility for what's going on, taking charge and finding solutions to problems."

"You really think that's what Lisa wants? Do you really think it would make a difference?"

"Michael, once I learned this, Grandma started respecting me more, even when she disagreed with me."

"She didn't see you as controlling?"

"If she wanted something a certain way, and I was against it just to be bossy – then that would be controlling. If I had insisted on something that showed I cared only about myself – that would be controlling. But when you set a goal that shows you care about your loved ones and you stick to it even when people are against you, that's being strong."

"What did you do?"

"I'll teach you. Listen."

> *Being strong isn't easy. It's taking responsibility for what's going on, taking charge and finding solutions.*

CHAPTER SIX

Listening

Grandpa and Michael walked along the wooded ridge to a clearing where an old fire lookout tower used to be. "When I started coming to this park, the lookout tower was still here," Grandpa remembered. "That's how the mountain got its name. The lookout in the tower watched for forest fires and called for help when he saw one."

A platform had replaced the lookout tower. They climbed the wooden steps to the top. Michael was awed by the spectacular view of mountains, lakes and forest in every direction. He hated to break the perfect silence, but after a moment, he said, "I thought it was important to listen to your wife and that you should each make decisions."

"Of course you should. Do you think that's a new idea?"

"I think so," Michael shrugged.

Grandpa looked through his notebook. "In the valley of the Tigris and Euphrates rivers in southwestern Asia was the land of Babylonia. The ancient Greeks called it Mesopotamia. It's now Iraq. In the third century, there was a popular saying in Babylonia, 'If your wife is short, bend down and seek her advice.'[14] In other words, make an effort to listen to what she says."

Michael looked surprised.

"A group of teachers in Babylonia wrote that in some matters, a man should make the decisions, and in some, the woman should decide. They said a woman's advice is invaluable, but Michael, that doesn't mean that every matter is one your wife decides. One of the teachers added that you should be careful not to hurt your wife's feelings, but if you always automatically follow her advice without using your own judgement, your life can become hell. She may lead you to do something wrong."[15]

Grandpa continued, "Grandma is a smart person. I value and appreciate her advice, but I don't always just do whatever she says."

"They said that in the third century?" Michael was surprised. "That's almost two thousand years ago. I thought men ruled the roost back then."

"Really?" Grandpa said as he turned a page. "Two thousand years ago they also said there are three lives that are not lives – one is the person who needs to eat at another's table in order to live, another is a person whose body is racked with pain.[16] Do you know what's the other life that isn't a life?"

"What?"

"A man whose wife rules over him."[17]

Michael was stunned as if something had hit him. "That's how I feel, like I don't have a life. How come nobody told me this? I thought things were different then."

"Human nature hasn't changed."

"But Grandpa, what you're reading is men telling other men about women."

Grandpa shook his head and leafed through the notebook. "What's wrong with men giving other men advice about being a man? We've been doing it for a long time. I'm glad we're finally talking about it. Do you want a woman to tell you? I heard what Leanna said at breakfast. She doesn't want a man who says, 'You decide.'"

"True," Michael reflected.

Grandpa continued, "I learned that to be strong meant I

had to be open and listen to Grandma's ideas, and use my own judgement. Sometimes I had to be flexible and compromise. Other times, I had to be firm. I couldn't give in on things I knew were wrong. And Michael, it's those difficult times when being strong and confident really matters."

Be careful not to hurt your wife's feelings, but if you're always led by her advice without using your own judgement, life can become hell. She may lead you to do something wrong, advised a teacher in the third century.

CHAPTER SEVEN

Being worthy

From the platform, Michael gazed over the vast expanse of forest. He watched the birds flying over the treetops below. "There's Crystal Lake. It seems so small from up here."

"Look!" Grandpa pointed upward to a bald eagle soaring in the sky.

"It's so powerful and graceful – look at it go," Michael stared at the bird.

As the eagle flew out of sight, Michael turned to Grandpa. "If I were strong like an eagle," Michael laughed, "would Lisa go along with me? I don't think so – she's always flying off in the opposite direction."

"Michael, what you're saying isn't new. It's been going on for thousands of years."

"I know, you keep saying that."

"Remember Adam?"

"From the Bible? I'm not into religion, Grandpa."

"It doesn't matter. I want to show you that it isn't new. If these ideas have been around for thousands of years, I think they're worth looking at. A gust of wind turned the pages in Grandpa's notebook. He turned several more and found the one he wanted, "Adam was alone. He wanted a wife. And Eve was created to be a 'helper opposing him.'"[18]

Michael was puzzled. "'A helper opposing him?' What's that supposed to mean?"

"Good question. A commentator who lived in eleventh-century France wrote that it teaches us, 'If you're worthy, the woman will be a helper; if you're not worthy, she will be against you.'[19] In other words, it's up to you and me to make things work."

"Worthy? Grandpa, if you ask Lisa if I'm worthy, she'll say no. She's always against me."

"In the sixteenth century, a sage in Prague wrote, 'Man and woman are two opposites. If man is worthy, they merge into a unified whole. But if he is not worthy, she will be against him because they are opposites.'"[20]

Michael sighed. "Okay, Grandpa, how do I get Lisa to think I'm worthy?"

"Becoming stronger and stepping forward to handle things helped Grandma see me as worthy and she became my partner. The first step was I had to decide I was entitled to someone who's a helper and not against me."

It's up to you to make things work.

CHAPTER EIGHT

Being entitled

Grandpa and Michael climbed down from the lookout and continued walking until they came to an unmarked fork in the trail.

"Let's go this way. It's flatter ground," Grandpa suggested.

"I know these trails," Michael answered. "That route is easy, but it doesn't lead anywhere. The other way is harder, but it'll get us to the top."

Michael led Grandpa along the ridge to a high waterfall. The sound of water pounding onto rocks in the valley below echoed loudly. They stopped to savor the view.

Grandpa reflected, "One summer, Grandma and I rented a cottage near the park. We invited our friends Jim and Sharon and their kids to visit. Jim had trouble with my directions and they got lost. He had to stop at a cottage to ask the way. Sharon criticized him mercilessly in front of the kids for getting lost."

"Sounds familiar."

"I remember asking him, 'Don't you feel you should be treated better?'"

"What did he say?"

"He said that's the way Sharon is and there's no changing her. I told him maybe that was the best he thought he deserved."

Grandpa then turned a few pages in his notebook and read, "Three thousand years ago, King Solomon said, 'As a man thinks in his heart, so is he.'[21] You create your own world by what you do and what you don't do. I told Jim that if he believed he was entitled to better treatment, he'd get it."

"What could he do?"

"I told him, 'If you want Sharon to stop being so critical, you've got to act like you're entitled to being treated better and won't accept anything less. You set the limits.'"

Michael listened.

Grandpa continued, "I learned that change takes time. I

also realized that if I didn't stop Grandma from treating me badly, our bond would be lost. The more she treated me badly, the more she resented me. How could she respect me, if I didn't respect myself?"

"Grandpa, Lisa already resents me. It may be too late for us."

"It's easier to set a good pattern at the beginning when you're both most committed, but I don't think it's ever too late. If I could change my situation, you can change yours."

"How?" Michael asked.

Grandpa smiled, "Imagine a co-worker wants you to help him steal from the company. Would you do it?"

"Of course not."

"What if he pressured you, would you do it?"

"No. Never."

"Would you yell at him?"

"There's no need. I'd just tell him there's no way."

"Here's another situation. You're out with your son Danny and he wants you to buy him something. You've already bought him a few things and you say you'll get it for him next time. But Danny wants it now and starts throwing a tantrum. Would you let him act that way? Would you give in? Would you get angry?"

"No. I'd tell him if he continues, he won't get it next time either. He'd stop pretty fast because he knows I mean what I say."

"Michael, when you're certain something is not acceptable, you know how to calmly set the limits on how others treat you."

"True."

"When I saw how Sharon treated Jim, I thought how could he let her treat him that way? Then I thought of the things that I let go on and asked myself the same question. I realized that if I didn't believe I was entitled to better treatment, I wouldn't get it either."

"Okay Grandpa, what do I do when Lisa tells me over and over to do something when I've already told her I'll do it, but not right now?"

"Grandma was also like that. I told her I already said when I'd do it and that if she didn't stop asking me, I wouldn't do it at all. She stopped and I made sure I kept my word."

"It worked?"

"Yes, but you have to be consistent in what you're willing to accept," Grandpa answered. "Michael, think about your son. You're a role model for him. What kind of man do you want him to be? How do you want women to treat him? Think about your daughter. Girls often marry men who are like their fathers. You have to be the kind of man you want your daughter to choose."

Michael nodded. "Good point."

When you believe you're entitled to being treated well, you won't accept anything less. If you wait until things are very bad, it means you've set the limit too low.

CHAPTER NINE

Taking full responsibility

Michael and Grandpa were close to the summit. Just before the top, the trail dropped steeply, forcing them to slow down and keep their eyes on the ground so they wouldn't trip over rocks or exposed tree roots.

"I used to think hiking up a mountain was harder than going down," Michael said. "But when you're actually doing it, going downhill is harder."

"When you're used to seeing things a certain way," said Grandpa, "it's hard to look at them differently. I'll give you an example. I used to blame Grandma for the way things were between us. I'd blame her upbringing – that way I could blame her parents too. Other times, I'd blame her friends for influencing her."

"I do that, but it's true. Lisa acts the way she does because of her parents and what her friends tell her."

"But, Michael, I couldn't change Grandma's upbringing or what her friends were telling her. I had to learn to see things another way. I had to look at my own actions. What was I doing? How was I handling it? The only behavior I could change was my own. Grandma was responding to what I was doing – or what I wasn't doing and should have been doing."

"Hmm. Maybe it worked for you, but you don't understand – Lisa is a special case."

"I thought Grandma was a special case. Everybody thinks their situation is special."

"But mine really is."

"Being strong meant I had to take full responsibility for making things better. I had to take action to achieve what I wanted. I couldn't keep saying, 'She has to change,' and then wait for her to change. Taking full responsibility also meant that I couldn't give in to her on something that I knew was wrong and then turn around and blame her when things went wrong."

"Good point," Michael said.

"I also learned I wasn't the first one to make this mistake."

Michael interrupted, "I know – you're going to say it's been going on for thousands of years."

Grandpa laughed. "Do you know who did it first?"

"I don't, but I know you're going to tell me." Michael smiled as he and Grandpa sat down on a fallen tree trunk.

Grandpa thumbed through his notebook. "Remember Adam and Eve? They were in the Garden of Eden. It was paradise. They're commanded not to eat the fruit from the Tree of Knowledge. What happens? Eve eats it and then gives some to Adam. What does he do? He did what you and I probably would have done. He went along with her. He ate the fruit."

"I know the story." Michael grinned.

"But what happens when Adam is asked if he ate the forbidden fruit? Does he take responsibility for what he did?"

Michael wasn't sure.

"He says, 'Eve gave it to me.'[22] He blames his wife. And what happens? They're both punished."

"Why was Adam punished? It's true. Eve gave him the fruit to eat."

"That's exactly why he was punished." Grandpa turned to another page in his notebook. "It's because he listened to his wife's voice[23] and didn't do what he knew was right. In seventeenth-century Italy, a commentator wrote that Adam was punished for blindly taking his wife's advice."[24]

Michael shook his head. "Sounds like me. So many times, I've given in to Lisa for the sake of peace, thinking she's going to appreciate me for it. Then, when it turns out badly, just like I thought it would, I blame her."

Grandpa could see Michael's frustration. "Don't be so hard on yourself. It happens to a lot of us."

"When it says Adam gave in to Eve's voice, what was her voice like? Was she seductive?"

Grandpa turned a page in his notebook. "There's an explanation that says Adam didn't know which fruit Eve offered him because she gave him juice she had squeezed from the fruit. When he hesitated, she argued with him, but she still couldn't get him to have it. Then she screamed till he couldn't take it any more and he did what she wanted."

"Has nothing changed? Lisa keeps at me until I can't stand it any more and I give in."

"We used to call it nagging," Grandpa chuckled.

Michael laughed uncomfortably. "Lisa says she's trying to communicate with me."

"You've taught Lisa how to get what she wants from you."

"Is it my fault? I couldn't take it," Michael sighed in frustration.

"I'm not blaming you – I'm telling you that you have to know what you want and you are responsible for changing the situation. Nobody wants to hear you complain that you're a victim of Lisa. How do you react when you hear a man complain about a woman treating him badly? Don't you think it's unmanly?"

"What can I do?"

"First, ask yourself why you give in. Does it make you feel needed? Do you want her approval? I had to learn to say no, politely, firmly and confidently. I'd have a picture in my mind of Grandma respecting me and looking up to me – even when I didn't do what she wanted. I kept that picture in my mind even if she raised her voice at me. She didn't change overnight, but it worked sooner than I thought."

Michael was becoming restless. He stood up and Grandpa followed him down the path.

Stop blaming others. Take full responsibility for changing the situation. The only person's behavior you can change is your own. Realize that she responds to what you do or don't do.

CHAPTER TEN

Growing stronger

They reached the summit of Lookout Mountain. Michael looked out over clear lakes, vibrant green forest and endless blue sky. He proposed a toast, "To reaching the top. We set our goal and we did it." They drank from their canteens and sat down on a large rock.

Once Michael got comfortable, he continued, "Grandpa, I'm grateful for what Lisa does, but when I try to take charge, she criticizes me. If she wants me to be strong, then why is she trying to control me? If I give in to be nice, she resents me."

Grandpa laughed, "I didn't get it either. Then I learned there is a purpose."

Michael snickered. "Sure, there's a purpose. She does it to get her way."

"She may be testing you, to see how strong you are, to see if you have backbone. If you don't have backbone, she'll resent you. I learned that if I gave in to manipulation, she despised me for not being strong. If you don't have backbone, it means you're not strong enough to protect her – and she wants to feel protected."

Grandpa turned a few pages in his notebook. "In eighteenth century Italy, a mystic wrote that everything that happens to us in life is a trial, a test we should see as an opportunity to grow, as something pushing us to find strength we didn't know we had. The bigger the test, the more we're pushed to grow."[25]

Grandpa put down the notebook and said, "When I read that, I knew it applied to me. I could see a lot of the situations that happened were tests. I had to become stronger and more confident, and I learned that I could be stronger and more sure of myself than I thought."

Grandpa drank more water from his canteen. "Michael, what kind of people do we usually admire? People who overcome hardship and become stronger and more self-assured for it. People who know what they want and take action to make their lives the way they want them to be. People who don't make excuses and blame others."

Michael listened closely, then said, "But I feel like a victim."

"Michael, think of it as a mirror. The things that bothered me were telling me how I needed to grow. The criticizing and controlling were going on because I needed to become stronger and have more confidence. I learned the fear of being criticized holds a lot of people back from taking initiative — initiative that would help them grow stronger."

"I'm surprised to hear you say that. I always thought you were strong."

"I pushed myself until it became part of me. If you act like a victim and blame the other person, you're missing an opportunity to grow."

"I understand what you're saying, but it's still Lisa's fault for acting the way she does."

"Fault doesn't matter. I had to change because I didn't like what was going on. I could see everybody's shortcomings but my own. It was hard to see that I was contributing to the problem. It was easier to see what Grandma was doing and blame her, but she wasn't the villain and neither was I. We each were a mirror of how the other person needed to grow. Grandma is my mirror. Lisa is yours."

"But I get along with everybody – except Lisa."

"Of course. Nobody knows Grandma better than I do, and she knows me better than anybody else. It means we know each other's shortcomings better than anybody. I heard a woman say, 'You think my husband is nice? You don't know him like I do.' It's true, few people know your faults like Lisa does. But it's because she knows you so well that she can help you grow."

"It's not easy."

Grandpa leaned back against a tree trunk. "Years ago, I worked for a company that sold cheese to grocery stores. I was paid on commission. The cheeses were delicious, but I didn't sell anything for the first three months. I was worried about how we'd pay our bills. I blamed the people who did the buying for the stores. It had to be their fault because they wouldn't listen to me. Grandma suggested I watch other salespeople and learn as much as I could. I started doing things differently and that's when I started selling. If I'd kept trying to sell the old way, things never would have changed. Changing the way I acted changed the situation."

When she opposes you, she may be testing to see if you're strong and know what you want. It's an opportunity to push yourself to grow as a person. The bigger the challenge, the more you're pushed to grow.

CHAPTER ELEVEN

Being manly

After resting at the summit, Grandpa and Michael started the walk down Lookout Mountain. They hiked along a ridge that dropped gradually and soon reached Sapphire Lake. Michael looked at the narrow lake and admired its breathtaking turquoise color. The shore they walked along was covered with smooth flat stones. Michael picked up a stone and tossed it onto the lake. It skipped along the water four times and then skimmed on the surface before it sank.

"I remember when I figured out the secret of making

stones skip," Michael said. "You have to put a spin on it as you throw it – otherwise, it sinks."

Grandpa tossed a stone. It skipped twice, glided on the water and then went under.

Grandpa smiled, "I learned another secret."

Michael laughed and said, "What's the secret?"

"Being manly."

"But, I've heard it over and over. Women don't like men who are macho."

"You're putting the wrong spin on it. I didn't say macho. I said manly."

Grandpa turned a page in his notebook and read, "What does it mean to be manly? To be manly is to have the noble qualities of a man who is of mature character.[26] It means to have the admirable traits and virtues of being honorable, having courage and being independent.[27] According to the Oxford English Dictionary, these meanings date from the thirteenth century.[28] For hundreds of years, that's what people meant when they talked about being manly."[29]

"Noble qualities? That's not what I hear people say about being manly," Michael said. He tossed another rock onto the lake. It skipped only once before it sank.

"Tell them to look it up in the Oxford English Dictionary," Grandpa said. "When I learned this, I made it my goal to be more of what it really means to be manly."

Grandpa read again from his notebook. "To be of mature character is to have high moral qualities, self-discipline, decisiveness and strength in your convictions. To be honorable is to be worthy of being honored, to be honest and have integrity. To have courage is to be able to deal with difficulty, pain or danger without backing away – despite your fear. And to be independent is to be confident and self-reliant," Grandpa finished reading.

Michael replied, "These days, I don't hear people say virtues and men in the same breath."

Grandpa laughed. "Michael, one of the meanings of the word virtue is manly strength and courage. Two thousand years ago, when the Romans used the word virtus, which is Latin for virtue, they meant manliness."[30]

Michael tossed one last stone onto the lake. It skipped five times before it sank.

Being manly means having high moral standards, being self-disciplined, being decisive, having strength in your convictions, being honest and having the courage to face difficulties. It's being confident and self-reliant.

CHAPTER TWELVE

Giving

Michael and Grandpa walked along the shore of Sapphire Lake until they reached a small log house known as the Artist's Cabin. Michael could see why a group of landscape painters had picked this spot to build a cabin for their painting trips in the park. From the front door, he had a spectacular view of Sapphire Lake and the valley.

"Look over there Grandpa – that's where we started hiking. There's a saying: The longest journey begins with a single step. We've come a long way, let's rest here."

Michael and Grandpa went inside the cabin and sat at a wooden table. Michael handed Grandpa a bag of nuts and raisins.

"You're giving some snacks to your grandpa? Thanks."

"I like to give, Grandpa. I give Lisa a lot and I don't ask for much in return. I thought love meant giving. But she's not happy."

"Michael, I used to think that if I gave everything I could to another person, that person would love me in return. Then I learned that we tend to love the people we give to – more than the people we receive from. The more you give, the more your love grows. Don't you feel this when you give to your children – the more you do for them, the more you love them?"

"That's true," Michael said.

"But do all children whose parents gave them a lot, love their parents?" Grandpa asked.

"Sometimes the kids who received a lot seem to resent their parents the most," Michael answered.

"How many men do you know, who worked hard to pay for all the things their wives wanted – and their wives are unhappy and the men can't understand why?"

"Too many," Michael said, shaking his head.

Grandpa opened his notebook. "'Love flows in the direction of giving.'[31] That was written by Eliyahu Dessler, a teacher of ethical behavior in England in the 1930s."

"He wrote, 'Love and giving come together.' He said we might think loving leads to giving because we see people giving to someone they love, but it's the other way around. 'The one who gives, loves.' People love what they have nurtured. They see a part of themselves in who they give to."[32]

Michael listened carefully.

"Why doesn't love seem to last?[33] Dessler said people tend to be takers, not givers. When two people are strongly attracted to one another, they become givers and lovers. Remember how you looked for ways to give to each other when you first became a couple?"

"Yes, I do. What happened?"

"Dessler said that after a while, those strong feelings lose their grip and people relapse into being takers. It's a subtle change. At the beginning, there is love and giving. Gradually, they go back to being takers and each starts making demands on the other. He said, 'When demands begin, love departs.' He advised couples to 'strive to keep the desire to give to each other fresh and strong.'"[34]

"I think I'm beginning to understand what you're talking about. Nobody ever told me this before."

Grandpa put down the notebook and said, "I learned that it's important that I give to Grandma – including giving her attention and gifts, so my feelings of love would keep growing. I also had to learn to let her give to me – not so that I could take – but so her feelings of love could grow and I could show her how much I appreciate her."

"I never thought of it that way."

"At breakfast, when Grandma served me first, you looked at us like we were so old-fashioned."

"My face showed it?" Michael was surprised. "When we were first married, Lisa used to make my lunch for me to take to work, but I didn't like the way she made it. It was easier for me to make it myself."

Grandpa turned another page and read, "Samson Raphael Hirsch wrote that even if a wife has servants, she should never leave others to 'perform attentions' that show her feelings of caring for her husband.[35] Even if you don't like a person, by helping and doing things for him, you'll start to change your feelings toward him."[36]

"It's hard."

"Yes, it is," Grandpa replied, "but we have to force ourselves to do it. If you feel like holding back, make yourself run to do it."

"It's not that easy."

"The opposite is also true. Treating someone badly will make you dislike that person. If you let Lisa treat you badly, she won't love you for it. She's going to start disliking you, and that can grow into hatred. How can she love someone who lets himself be treated badly?"[37]

Michael said uncomfortably, "I'm listening to you, Grandpa, but I'm not sure that I agree with everything you've said."

"Love and giving come together," *Eliyahu Dessler said. People develop feelings of love for those to whom they give. Problems often begin when people go from being givers to being takers.*

CHAPTER THIRTEEN

Setting goals

Grandpa heard the loud honking of geese. "Look," he said, pointing out the door of the cabin. Overhead, geese flew in V formation. "They're returning from their winter migration."

"Grandpa, do you know why geese fly in a V when they're migrating?"

"Why?"

"As each bird flaps its wings, it provides lift for the birds following it. It helps them get farther, using less energy."

"Interesting, but it only works because they're all going the same way," Grandpa smiled. "Are you and Lisa going the same way? What goals do you both have? After fifty years, what do you want to have accomplished?"

"I haven't thought that far ahead."

"You have to know what you want and have a plan to get there.

At the beginning, Grandma and I talked about our goals. And I learned that we had to keep talking about them. We talked about how we wanted to live and raise our children, how we were going to earn money and how we were going to spend it. Do you ever discuss goals with Lisa?"

"At first we did."

Grandpa drank some water. "Having goals gave us a purpose that helped keep us going in hard times. If we hadn't felt we had important goals to accomplish, we probably would have given up. If your only goal is love, what will keep you together when feelings of love aren't that strong?"

Michael listened.

"I learned to picture what we wanted and make a plan on how to get there. Our goals helped guide me when I had to make decisions. People are more likely to accept something they might not want at first if they see it as part of the whole picture. Without goals to guide me, I would have been pulled all over the place."

Think about what you want to accomplish and plan how you're going to get there.

Talk about each other's goals. They give purpose that can keep a couple together in hard times.

CHAPTER FOURTEEN

Knowing what's going on

Grandpa continued, "To be able to guide my family, I needed to know what was going on in their lives. I learned to pay close attention to what was happening. I listened carefully to Grandma and the kids when they spoke. I made an effort to understand how they felt. I asked them about their activities and what they were thinking about and how they were feeling. I asked about things that they had told me. It showed I was listening when they'd spoken to me before. If I saw something was bothering them, I listened. I gave them the attention they needed. They knew I cared about them."

"I try to do that – when I'm not being undermined," Michael said.

"By knowing what was going on, I knew when I needed to take charge of a situation and find solutions. Before I learned that, Grandma would accuse me of leaving everything to her."

"Lisa says I leave everything to her. Is that what she means? Grandpa, I'm starting to understand what you're saying."

"When Grandma saw I knew what was going on and I took the initiative to deal with things, she was less critical. If I waited for her to take the first step, then contradicted her, she'd say I was interfering."

"I can relate to that," Michael said.

"When people feel that you care about them, they're more likely to accept your guidance. There's an old saying: People don't care how much you know until they know how much you care."

Michael smiled. "That's how I feel about you, Grandpa. You always took an interest in me when I was growing up. You were the only adult who listened. I felt you cared about me. I guess that's why I'm talking with you now."

Michael hugged his grandfather, and said, "So, Grandpa, what's next?"

*Know what's going on, so you know
when you need to take charge
and find solutions.*

*People don't care how much you
know until they know how
much you care. When you take an
interest in someone's life, that
person feels you care and is often
more willing to listen to
your guidance.*

CHAPTER FIFTEEN

Think before you act

Grandpa opened his notebook and said, "There's a Chinese proverb: 'The family man should govern his family as you would cook a small fish – very carefully.'"[38]

Michael laughed.

Grandpa continued, "Think carefully before you do anything. Don't just react. Don't just follow your emotions." He glanced at his notebook and said, "One of the meanings of being strong is being 'able to think vigorously and clearly.'[39] I learned to plan how I would deal with situations

– especially situations that already happened and I knew would happen again."

"What do I do about Lisa undermining me in front of our kids?"

Grandpa paused and said, "Don't step back, don't withdraw. When Grandma would undermine me, I asked for her support. I'd say, 'Please support me with the children. If you disagree with me, tell me later – but not in front of the children.'"

Michael listened.

"It's not easy," Grandpa said as he looked in his notebook. "Michel de Montaigne was a philosopher and a mayor of Bordeaux in sixteenth-century France.[40] He said, 'Governing a family is hardly less challenging than governing a whole kingdom.'"[41]

Michael smiled.

"I realized I had to take the initiative and make things happen. One of the most important things I learned was to have confidence in my own ideas."

A red squirrel had slipped into the cabin and was trying to get into Grandpa's knapsack. Michael chased it away. The squirrel darted up a rafter and scolded Michael with loud chattering.

Grandpa laughed. "The squirrel made my point. I learned to speak up, so people would know what I was thinking. I couldn't expect them to read my mind. I couldn't say they should have known. Sometimes, when I was alone, I'd practice saying my thoughts out loud, so I'd sound confident when I spoke."

Grandpa continued, "I also made sure I stood up straight – it shows you're strong. If you don't feel strong, stand up straight and put your shoulders back. You'll feel your backbone. I also avoided words that showed lack of confidence – like 'sort of' or 'kind of.' I made sure I was always definite and positive."

Grandpa turned a page in his notebook. "Moses Maimonides was a physician and philosopher in twelfth-century Spain. He wrote that a man should speak pleasantly and gently to his wife. He shouldn't be sad or quick to anger.[42] I learned to always look for the good things about Grandma that I could praise. I want to show her that I appreciate her," Grandpa smiled.

"Even for things she's supposed to do?" Michael asked.

"Of course. The more she sees that I appreciate her, the happier she is. Everybody wants to be appreciated. Don't you want Lisa to appreciate you?"

"Sure I do."

"I learned to criticize only when it was really necessary. I also learned to control my temper. People get angry when they don't know how to handle a situation and don't know what else to do. Getting angry is the opposite of being strong. You can do a lot of damage to yourself and others. She'll remember hurtful words for a long time. I learned that before I did anything, I had to stop and think about how I could handle things calmly."

"How is getting angry the opposite of being strong?" Michael asked.

Grandpa looked in his notebook. "In the second century, a teacher named Ben Zoma said, 'Who is strong? He who controls his emotions.' He quoted King Solomon, who a thousand years earlier wrote, 'He who is slow to anger is better than the strong man, and a master of his passions is better than a conqueror of a city.'[43] I learned that if you can overcome your anger, you're stronger than the person who can conquer others but can't control his own anger."

"What if it's your nature to get angry?" Michael asked.

"You can control how you react. Imagine you're yelling at someone. The telephone rings. It's your boss. How fast do you calm down? Pretty fast, or else you'd lose your job. Do you know the story of the scorpion and the frog?"

"No, tell me."

"A scorpion and a frog wanted to cross a river. The scorpion asked the frog, 'Please take me on your back while you swim across the river.' The frog replied, 'I'm afraid you'll sting me.' The scorpion said, 'If I sting you, we'll both drown.' So the frog let the scorpion get on his back and started swimming across the river. In the middle, the scorpion stings the frog and they both start to go under. The surprised frog said, 'How could you? You're going to drown too.' The scorpion replied, 'I can't help it. It's my nature.'"[44]

Michael laughed.

Grandpa said, "People aren't scorpions. We can control our actions."

Think before you do anything. Don't just react and follow your emotions. Anticipate situations and plan how to handle them calmly.

Getting angry damages you and other people. It shows you don't know how to handle the situation.

CHAPTER SIXTEEN

Making decisions

Grandpa continued, "To be strong and confident, you have to make decisions and take responsibility for them. I learned I had to be more decisive and that I was responsible for the outcome."

"I try to be decisive, but with the way things are, it's hard."

"To Grandma, if I avoided making decisions, I was avoiding my responsibilities. It's hard work to make decisions and take responsibility for them. If I said to her, 'You decide,'

I was stepping back when I should have been stepping forward. She felt very frustrated with me. She felt I wasn't protecting her."

Michael smiled. "I hadn't thought of it that way."

"Sometimes you have to make decisions that people don't like, and they get angry, but you have to do it. Everybody who makes decisions has to deal with people who don't like the decisions. I learned that I had to try and understand their feelings. I had to help them see the good in decisions they didn't like. I'd try to make them feel good about doing things they didn't want to do. It's not easy, but if you avoid difficult decisions, you're not dealing with things that need to be dealt with, and Lisa is going to resent you."

"Grandpa, she already does."

"You can change that."

"If I make bad decisions, she blames me."

"I learned to trust my judgement. It's often better to make a bad decision than to make no decision. I used to think that if I avoided making a decision, then I could avoid being blamed for a bad decision. Then I realized that I still didn't avoid the consequences of not making a decision."

"Sometimes I don't know what to decide," Michael said.

"Learn as much as you can. There are a lot of sources of information. Ask for different opinions."

"I've done that. And when Lisa pressures me to do something I know is wrong, what do I do? It's hard for me to say no to her."

"What matters is not what you do when everyone agrees with you – it's what you do when people don't agree with you. You can't please everybody all the time. Leadership means making choices that some people are going to disagree with. I had to know what my values are. When my decisions were guided by my values, I wasn't easily swayed. It gave me strength and confidence in my convictions. It made me more resilient to criticism."

"If I don't do what Lisa wants, she accuses me of all kinds of things."

"When I make a decision, I look at the possible results. I think about tomorrow, not just about today. I listen to what Grandma says. I talk to her and make sure I understand her opinion and her reasons. Sometimes she wants to keep me from acting rashly. Sometimes she makes me aware of things I hadn't thought of, and I agree with her. By disagreeing with me, she helps me – and I'd change my mind or we'd compromise. Being flexible takes strength and confidence too. But if it's something I can't honestly compromise on, I stand firm."

"Grandpa, don't decisions sometimes just make themselves?"

"I used to think that. It's a way of avoiding responsibility. I started giving myself a deadline to decide. Without it, I could drift for a long time."

"And if I make a bad decision, one that affects people's lives?" Michael asked.

"You made a mistake. Taking responsibility for it is a sign of strength."

"It's not easy."

"Who should make those decisions – someone who isn't afraid of making mistakes?" Grandpa said as he turned a page in his notebook. "Napoleon Bonaparte said, 'Nothing is more difficult, and therefore more precious, than to be able to decide.'"[45]

"That's interesting," Michael said.

"I learned that the decisions I made in difficult times counted the most with Grandma. It was when things were hard that she most wanted to look up to me. Think about it – when there's a crisis, we respect people who have the confidence to take charge. We don't admire people who stand back."

*If you avoid making decisions —
by letting others decide or by
delaying until the decision
makes itself — she may feel you're
avoiding your responsibilities.
Being strong means stepping
forward to make decisions in
difficult situations and taking
responsibility for the outcome.*

CHAPTER SEVENTEEN

Watch men who are strong

"I learned a lot by watching men who are strong. I watched how they act with confidence, and how they take charge. I saw that they didn't try to please everyone. They know that sometimes they have to make a decision that others are against. I also saw how their wives admired them when they took charge."

"I thought those kind of men were out of date," Michael asked. "I'm not comfortable being around them."

"It's easier to choose friends who are like us. But I learned that when I'm uncomfortable with someone, it may mean there's something I can learn from him. I not only watched men who were strong, I became friends with them, so I could learn by being with them."

"Grandpa, Lisa gave me such a hard time just because I wanted to spend time with you today," Michael said, exasperated. He paused for a moment and said, "When I think about the couples Lisa and I are friends with – the men are a lot like me."

Grandpa answered, "When I watched men who were strong, I started picturing myself being like them. I let that picture influence the way I acted. I would ask myself, how would a man who is strong act?"

"Interesting."

Grandpa turned a page in his notebook, and said, "It's not new. In the fourth century, a teacher advised husbands to 'go up a step' and associate with men who are good examples.[46] By watching men who were strong, I began to catch myself if I started to step back. When I felt unsure of myself, I'd force myself to act strong and confident. I'd say to myself: 'She wants me to be strong. Take a deep breath and do it.' The more I acted strong and confident on the outside, the stronger and more confident I became inside."

"There have been decisions that were important to me, but when I tried to take charge, Lisa ignored me, and we got into a big argument," Michael said.

"She isn't used to you stepping forward. Change takes time."

"What if she keeps ignoring me?"

"I used to think that Grandma would ignore me because in my mind I didn't really expect her to go along with me. And when she didn't, I accepted it. I had to change the picture in my mind. I had to expect her to respond positively. It took time, but gradually she changed the way she reacted to me."

Michael thought about what Grandpa was saying. Why hadn't he thought of it before? He asked, "How do I apply this to what Lisa and I argue about?"

Watch men who are strong.
Watch how they take charge.
Become friends with them.

Expect her to respond
positively to you.

CHAPTER EIGHTEEN

Money

"Like money?" Grandpa asked.

Michael nodded.

Grandpa laughed, "It's not new."

"I know, I know. Thousands of years ago they said – so tell me, what did they say?"

Grandpa opened his notebook and read, "In the third century, teachers taught how to avoid problems that lead to arguments at home. They said, 'Be careful with family finances, as quarrels are most common in homes where there is financial stress. Financial problems can bring out or aggravate problems in a marriage that would not have otherwise arisen.'"[47]

"That hits the nail on the head, doesn't it?" Michael said.

"They even discouraged people from making an investment if it could cause financial strain in the short run – even if in the long run, it could make a lot of money."[48] Grandpa continued.

"Hmm, interesting. That's a good point."

"I'm grateful that Grandma is careful with money. She doesn't buy things we can't afford. We don't live beyond our means. We learned to be happy with what we have."

Grandpa turned to another page in his notebook. "Remember Ben Zoma who wrote about 'Who is strong?' He also wrote, 'Who is rich? He who is happy with his share.'[49] The person who is truly wealthy is the person who is content with what he has."

Grandpa took a drink of water from his canteen. "I learned a lesson from my neighbors Bruce and Claire. They were always buying furniture, new cars – all kinds of things they didn't really need. I must admit, I did envy all the things they had. If I saw an ad for some new gadget, they soon had it. They were always buying, buying, buying, but it didn't look like it made them happy. They were always looking for more, as if that new thing would finally make them happy.

Eventually, they couldn't make their payments. Their cars were repossessed. I could hear them arguing. One day, Bruce told me he was jealous of me. He envied the peace in my home."

Michael sighed. "Lisa spends too much money. I tell her, but she doesn't stop. I had to get a job on the side so I can pay the bills. I can't keep going on like this."

"If you go broke because Lisa spends too much money, people are going to blame you. They'll say you weren't taking responsibility for the finances."

"But it's Lisa who's overspending."

"People don't want to hear a man say he's a victim of a woman. Men are expected to be strong. We're supposed to be able to deal with these things. And if we don't, we still get blamed."

"What do I do?"

"Michael, look at how you're handling it. You're letting it go on. Do you need to keep pleasing her by paying for things you can't afford? Does it make you feel needed? Being strong means knowing when and how to say no."

Grandpa turned another page in his notebook and read, "Akiva, a teacher in the second century, said that a man who gets rich so he can give his wife luxuries isn't rich, because his wife will never be satisfied. Akiva said, 'Who is truly rich? A man married to a wife whose ways are pleasant, who doesn't demand a lot of material things and who along with her husband appreciates what they have.'"[50]

Michael shook his head and said, "Grandpa, I can't get through to her."

"Michael, to change my situation I had to change what I did. That's what you have to do."

Be careful with money. Financial stress can bring out problems that would not have otherwise arisen.

Don't compete with others. Let them envy the peace in your home.

CHAPTER NINETEEN

The big house

Grandpa and Michael heard the rapid tapping of a woodpecker and walked over to an open window. The woodpecker was chiseling his way into a tree outside the cabin.

"Did you know that male woodpeckers carve a home in a tree to impress the female woodpecker?" Michael asked.

"Michael, we can learn from them. They build homes, but their homes are small holes in trees. They don't take on more house than they can handle."

"Interesting," Michael said. He thought about what had happened to a friend of his. "My friend Paul told me why he and his wife split up. Grandpa, it was as if we were with the same woman. She wanted a bigger house. He said they couldn't afford it. She said she'd go back to work to help pay for it. Once they bought the bigger house, she wouldn't go to work."

"What did Paul do about it?" Grandpa asked.

"I told you. They separated."

"And what are you going to do about it? Michael, too many people become slaves to paying for a big house. She might want a big house, but what you both need is a peaceful home. Don't buy more house than you can afford. It's better to have a small home that's calm, than a mansion where there's stress."

Grandpa read from his notebook, "Epictetus, a teacher in the second century, wrote, 'Just as you wouldn't choose to sail in a large and ornately decorated, gold-laden ship if you knew it was going to sink and you would drown, don't choose to live in a big expensive house if the result there is that you will be disturbed.'" [51]

"I told Lisa's father we were in over our heads financially because she wanted the bigger house. You know what he said? He said, 'It doesn't matter what Lisa wants. You're the man.'"

"He gave you good advice," Grandpa said. "Going along with your wife to buy a house you can't afford and then blaming her – sounds like what Adam did."

"I thought her father was old-fashioned, but now I see what he meant."

Grandpa paused and cleared his throat. "Let me tell you a story. A long time ago, there was a man who lived in a small hut – about the size of this cabin – with his wife and eight kids. They were always arguing. One day, he couldn't take it any more and went to his teacher for advice. 'We live in a small hut. We're always quarreling. Life is hard. What should I do?' The teacher asked him if he had a goat. The man was surprised and said he had three goats. The teacher told him to take one goat into his hut. The man was puzzled but he did what his teacher said."

"The hut was more cramped. A few days later, the man went back to his teacher and said, 'Life is harder. Please help us.' The teacher told him to take another goat into his hut."

"Life was worse. After a few days, he ran to his teacher and pleaded for help. The teacher told him to take the third goat into his hut. The man said, 'No more,' but the teacher insisted."

"There was more arguing than ever. A few days later, the man ran to his teacher and said 'We can't go on.' The teacher told him to let all the goats out of the hut. A few days later, he went to his teacher and said, 'My hut is so big. Life is good."

Don't get in over your head by buying more house than you can afford. It can cause enormous stress.

CHAPTER TWENTY

Working

"Do you know what caused arguments in my home?" Grandpa asked. "When the children were small, I wanted Grandma to stay home. I appreciated how hard she worked taking care of the kids. But as they got bigger, I needed Grandma to help bring in money, but she didn't want to."

"Sounds familiar, Grandpa. I thought I was being a good husband, working hard so Lisa could stay home with the kids. Now, I want her to go back to work, but she won't."

Grandpa nodded and said, "Sometimes in the afternoon I go to the gym to exercise. There are women going to fitness classes there. After the class, they go for a drink in the snack bar. I hear them complaining to each other about their husbands."

Michael laughed, "I thought only Lisa did that."

"Michael," Grandpa sighed as he turned a page in his notebook, "It's not new. In the twelfth century, Maimonides wrote that even if a man has a lot of money and his wife has many servants, she should not be idle, without work.[52] Even if you don't need the money, she still needs to be doing something productive."

Grandpa continued reading from his notebook, "Maimonides also said that if a woman wants to work and her husband doesn't want her to, the husband is wrong."[53]

"I thought the idea of women wanting to work started only a few decades ago."

"I told you, Michael. It's not new."

They heard the honking of geese flying overhead. Michael suddenly realized how much time had passed. "Grandpa, it's time to head back."

They hiked in silence along the trail. Michael thought about all the things his grandfather had said. It was so different from what he was used to hearing. Was it all old fashioned ideas? Or was Grandpa right – human nature hadn't changed? He wondered if it would work today. How would Lisa react?

It was dark by the time Grandpa and Michael reached the car. They could hear the cackling and hooting of an owl in the forest.

Michael started the car and drove out of the park. Grandpa soon fell asleep. As Michael drove back to the city, he thought about his life. Where was he heading if things with Lisa didn't change? He had friends who were divorced and he didn't want that.

As Michael drove into his grandparents' neighborhood, he slowed down and Grandpa woke up. Michael pulled into the driveway. Grandpa opened the car door and said, "Thanks for being the guide today. Don't spend too much time thinking about what I told you. Just try it and let me know how it goes."

In the twelfth century,
Maimonides wrote,
"Even if a man has a lot of
money and his wife
has many servants, she should
not be idle, without work."

CHAPTER TWENTY-ONE

This is what it's meant all along

Four months later, Michael, Lisa and their children Danny and Jessica went to visit Grandpa and Grandma. Michael looked relaxed, so did Lisa, who kept glancing at him and smiling. Grandma had baked shortbread cookies for the children. She loved watching the kids enjoy them. Before taking cookies for herself, Jessica offered some to her parents.

Michael joined Grandpa in his study. "How are things going with Lisa?" he asked.

"Better. I did what you said. I wasn't convinced it would work, but nothing else did, so I tried it. Every time I asked myself, 'What would Grandpa do in this situation?' And that's what I did."

"What happened?"

"I didn't tell her what I was doing. I just did it. Lisa seemed surprised at first. She argued, but I didn't give in. When she started pressuring me, I thought about what you'd said. She didn't let up. I thought it might be the end, but I was determined I had to change. Gradually, things improved. She started being happier. She stopped criticizing me. I began seeing the good person that Lisa is."

"That's great."

"I started telling my friends about it. You know what they said? They said what I said to you, that it sounds controlling. Then I had an idea."

"What?"

"I thought we needed a new word, so people wouldn't react with preconceived ideas. So I decided I'd make up a new word and give it my own meaning – like the people who came up with the word 're-engineering.'"

"What's the new word?"

"Husbandship, as in a man has to show husbandship."

"Hmm."

"Doesn't it sound like the right word?"

Grandpa nodded. "It's good."

"The first thing I did was look in a dictionary to see if it already existed."

Grandpa was curious. "Does it?"

"Yes, it does. Not only that, do you know what it means?"

"I can't guess. Tell me."

"It already means what I wanted it to mean." Michael took out his notebook, opened it and read, "Husbandship is the action of being a husband. Being a husband means being the male head of a household. It means someone who manages his household with skill and thrift. It's also a verb. To husband means to manage prudently and spend wisely and economically. Grandpa, the Oxford English Dictionary says this meaning dates from the eleventh century."[54]

"Interesting."

"Grandpa, it's not new. This is what it's meant to be a husband all along."

*This is what it's meant to be
a husband all along.
Remember, she wants to look
up to you. Start over and read
this story again.*

Notes

1. *What wives wish their husbands knew about women*, by Dr. James Dobson. Tyndale House Publishers, Wheaton, Illinois, 1975, page 102.

2. *The Life of Themistocles*, by A.J. Podlecki. McGill-Queen's University Press, Montreal, 1975.

3. *The Concise Columbia Dictionary of Quotations*, by Robert Andrews. Columbia University Press, New York, 1987, page 113.

4. *My Truth*, by Edda Mussolini Ciano, as told to Albert Zarca. William Morrow and Company, New York, 1977, page 40.

5. *The Wicked Wit of Winston Churchill*, compiled by Dominique Enright. Michael O'Mara Books Limited, London, 2001, page 107.

6. *Ibid.*, page 106.

7. Samson Raphael Hirsch, *Horeb* 80:525, translated from German by Dr. I. Grunfeld, Soncino Press, London, 1962, volume II, page 393.

8. *The Complete Artscroll Siddur.* Mesorah Publications Ltd., New York, 1984, page 811.

9. *Dr. Spock on Parenting*, by Benjamin Spock, M.D., Pocket Books, New York, 1989, pages 71 and 73.

10. *Ibid.*, page 76.

11. *Ibid.*

12. *Ibid.*

13. *Life Without Father*, by David Popenoe. The Free Press, New York, 1996, page 81.

14. *The Talmud*, The Steinsaltz Edition, commentary by Adin Steinsaltz, Volume 1, Tractate Bava Metzia, Part 1. Random House, New York, 1989, pages 59a and 231.

15. *Ibid.* See also *The Talmud*, The Schottenstein Edition, Tractate Bava Metzia. Mesorah Publications Ltd., New York, 1993, page 59a and footnote 14.

16. *The Talmud*, The Schottenstein Edition, *op. cit.*, Tractate Beitzah, page 32b.

17. *Ibid.*

18. *Genesis* 2:18.

19. *The Chumash*. Mesorah Publications Ltd., New York, 1993, page 13.

20. *Genesis*, Mesorah Publications Ltd., New York, 1977, volume 1, page 104.

21. *Proverbs* 23:7.

22. *Genesis* 3:12.

23. *Genesis* 3:17.

24. *The Chumash, op. cit.*, page 18.

25. *Table for Two: Making a good marriage better,* by Avraham Peretz Friedman. Targum/Feldheim, pages 17-18.

26. *Webster's New World Dictionary, College Edition.* Nelson Foster and Scott Ltd., Toronto, 1964, pages 887 and 893.

27. *Ibid.*

28. *The Oxford English Dictionary, Second Edition.* Clarendon Press, Oxford, United Kingdom, 1989, volume 9, page 322.

29. Recently published dictionaries may not include some of the more positive connotations of the word "manly." According to the publishers of the Merriam-Webster's

Collegiate Dictionary, the way in which "manly" is used changed in the latter half of the 20th century (correspondence with the publishers).

30. *Webster's New World Dictionary, op. cit.*, page 1630.

31. *Strive for Truth!* by Eliyahu Eliezer Dessler, translated by Aryeh Carmell. Feldheim Publishers, New York, 1978, Part One, page 129.

32. *Ibid.*, page 126.

33. *Ibid.*, page 132.

34. *Ibid.*

35. Hirsch, *op. cit.*, 81:538, page 401.

36. Dessler, *op. cit.*, pages 128-29.

37. *Ibid.*

38. *What is a man?* edited by Waller R. Newell. HarperCollins Publishers, New York, 2000, page 290.

39. *Webster's New World Dictionary, op. cit.*, page 1446.

40. "Montaigne, Michel Eyquem de," Microsoft®
    Encarta® *Online Encyclopedia* 2000
    http://encarta.msn.com © 1997-2000 Microsoft
    Corporation.

41. *What is a man? op. cit.*, page 290.

42. *The Code of Maimonides, Book Four,* 5:19, translated by
    Isaac Klein, Yale University Press, New Haven and
    London, 1972, page 98.

43. *Ethics of the Fathers* 4:1.

44. *Midrash Rabba,* Leviticus 22:4.

45. *Wisdom of the Generals,* by William A. Cohen, Ph.D,
    Prentice Hall Press, Paramus, NJ, 2001, page 44.

46. *The Babylonian Talmud,* Tractate Yebamoth, translated
    by Israel Slotki. Traditional Press, New York, page 63a
    and footnote 18.

47. *The Talmud,* The Steinsaltz Edition, *op. cit.,* Tractate Bava Metzia, page 59a.

48. *Ibid.*

49. *Ethics of the Fathers* 4:1.

50. *The Talmud,* The Schottenstein Edition, op. cit., Tractate Shabbos, page 25b and footnote 31.

51. *The Stoic Art of Living,* by Tom Morris, Open Court, Chicago, 2004, page 80.

52. *The Code of Maimonides,* 21:10, *op. cit.,* page 133.

53. *Ibid.,* 21:3, page 131.

54. *The Oxford English Dictionary, op. cit.,* volume 7, pages 510-512.

Share your story

If you have an experience or comments about *Being the Strong Man A Woman Wants* that you'd like to share, please go to www.beingthestrongman.com or e-mail: bethestrongman@aol.com

About the author

Seeking to understand the challenges he faced, Elliott Katz explored the wisdom of the ages. He discovered powerful, often-forgotten insights that gave him the answers he needed. He also discovered that many other people face similar challenges. People started seeking his advice and he was repeatedly told, "Why didn't someone tell me this before?"

Elliott Katz is a professional speechwriter and the author of seven non-fiction books including the bestseller *Great Country Walks Around Toronto*. He has written on a wide-range of subjects from the outdoors to the economy to how to stimulate ideas in the workplace. He teaches the principles in this book and is available to speak at seminars and conferences. Information: www.elliottkatz.com e-mail: bethestrongman@aol.com.

For others who could benefit

Elliott Katz is available to speak at seminars and conferences. (see About the Author)

This book is available at special quantity discounts for bulk purchases for educational purposes, premiums, sales promotions, fund-raising, special books or gift-giving.

Please send me _____ copies of *Being the Strong Man A Woman Wants*, at USA $12.95, Canada $14.95 plus 5% GST, and $4.00 per book for shipping and handling:

Award Press
www.awardpress.com
e-mail: bethestrongman@aol.com

Name: _____

Address: _____

_____

Telephone: _____ Fax: _____

E-mail _____

Your Notes

Your Notes

Your Notes